D1470427

The Meditation Manual

How to Master Meditation, Awaken Your Soul
& Transcend the Ego in One Week or Less

By: Koi Fresco

Other Books by Koi Fresco:
A (Not So) Enlightened Youth (2016)

Connect with Koi Fresco:
www.KoiFres.co
Youtube.com/KoisCorner
Instagram: @KoiFresco
Twitter: @KoiFresco

Table of Contents

"The mind become a monster when it becomes your master. The mind becomes an angel when it is your servant."

- Yogi Bhajan

"He who lives in harmony with himself, lives in harmony with the universe."

- Marcus Aurelius

*"Meditation is the way in which we come to feel our basic inseparability from the whole universe, and what that requires is that we **shut up**."*

- Alan Watts

Chapter 1

The Meditation Manual

What is Meditation?

Simple. That is what meditation is at its core. At face value it is merely the practice of holding complete awareness or focus on a single thought or frame of reference. In doing so such honed concentration has the potential to eventually allow any individual to enter into a space beyond thought entirely. A space of complete absorption in Ultimate Reality, in the True-Self that is beyond conception, beyond the body, and beyond the states of mind we currently witness life through. It doesn't matter if you are straight or gay, a lazy student or the boss of a successful business, a devout Christian or an adamant Atheist, white or black, these are all cast out in meditation.

Meditation is truly a practice for everyone. Therefore, in staying true to the spirit of meditation, this manual has been written with a foundation of simplicity as well. Not too long, not overly detailed, and above all, not too cluttered. While we will briefly discuss the philosophies & influences surrounding meditation and our true nature with the 'meditator' as our current roll. We will in turn discover more than just the roots of this ancient Eastern practice, but also that of its more recent influences on the body and brain. Yet beyond this we should all be here for one reason; To soak up the nectar of potentially mastering meditation with the assistance from five select methods I personally find necessary to the process of awakening. An awakening that not only ignites inner peace, but one that also shines am inextinguishable light on the internal and transcendental nature of what it means to be you, in a relatively short amount of time.

Thankfully this is a realization that surfaces most directly in personal meditative practice when done as part of our *sadhana* (daily spiritual practice). As well as when done an open heart full willing to discover the true depth that meditation holds.

While many modern spiritual movements might seem to contain dozens of highly complex steps and other-worldly theories ranging from the occult to aliens, you'll find no mention of those here. Furthermore, nothing to come in this manual is an isolated creation of my own. All of the wisdom to come is borrowed wisdom I have learned from my years of studies. These range from past civilizations, to siddhas, sages and scientists over many centuries of practice. All followed by millions of souls worldwide looking to find their own internal space of serenity. The purpose of this work is merely to simplify these often (unnecessarily) complex practices I have been taught, so that you too can reap the so-called 'rewards' of dedication and devotion to one of following methods. These ways of self-centering are ones that have been personally implemented into my life for many years, although hopefully once the practice is truly understood, a book such as this will become obsolete. Not to mention that the journey of making meditation second nature in the business of daily life can at times seem difficult depending on which book we pick up, or which teacher we decide to learn meditative methods from.

This in my experience has not only confused many people I have encountered during the countless guided meditation sessions and lectures I've held, but through hundreds emails as well. In essence difficult it the last thing we want when learning about inner peace, because most of us believe that from an outside perspective, that the primary function of reconnecting with our own true state of being should be simple! Which in truth, it is! So then, if this is in fact the case (as I claim it to be). So *why*, I am often asked, is there so much complexity surrounding meditation when we search for methods of learning? Well depending on who we pose this question to will always dictate the answer we receive. Which is often, in my humble opinion, unintentionally skewed in their own personal bias's favor. Some may say that the large amount of steps their method requires makes the meditative practice more fruitful, which in many cases is true. Others would argue that the history of their path is necessary and without it the practice is incomplete. Which may or may not be quite so true.

However regardless of cultural influences, alleged requirements and detailed histories of these many approaches to meditation, there exists one fundamental binding factor between them all; That beyond philosophies, beyond emotions and beyond the logical or empirical vantage we may try to apply to meditation, the ultimate goal (and subsequently the ultimate destination) is that of a *return* to a state of pure being-ness.

Meditation awakens a state beyond judgement, beyond expectation and most importantly beyond the current perceptions our identity defines life as. We are all playing out roles here within the confines of our ego-self's image. Meditation is the key to unlocking the door that allows one to step outside this shell we consider ourselves to be from the vantage we have been raised to view reality through, and instead become one with our True-Self. The universal whole. Meditation is the transcension of personal self, and it's partaking in the experiences of this play called human life. Thusly in moving beyond such states of thinking, it may just   drop us into a sea of pure awareness, which is in actuality a sea of pure cosmic bliss. The puppet becoming the puppeteer. The branch realizing it is in fact the entire tree. The human being seeing it is in actuality the entirety of the universe, watching itself from an illusory interior vantage of separateness.

In fact, our true state of being is what's known as *ananda* or true bliss in Hinduism. Existing not in a state of bliss during meditation but recognizing that we all, even in this moment, have the potential to live *as* bliss itself incarnate through consciousness. Always. It all just depends on how much we mature our practice, and how much our practice in turn matures us.

Now we might initially hear the word bliss and associate it to external influences that we assume create such a feeling. But this is a fleeting illusion. We might think of true bliss as kissing a lover, or visiting a theme park as a child, or even using chemical substances to alter our current state of mind, the way many people do to achieve a more expansive state of consciousness (if only for a short while). Still all of this is fickle in comparison to the true nature of bliss that sits dormant within you as it does within me.

To illustrate this point, imagine your favorite song. We might easily think that we *love* our favorite song. But in comparison to true unconditional love, maybe the love for a parent or a significant other, we recognize that what we consider 'love' for our favorite song is a misinterpretation of the word's true capability and meaning. What we actually mean is that we really, *really* like our favorite song, but we do not love it the way we love family or friends. One word, multiple levels of meaning. If we can understand this simple mistake, we can also apply this misinterpretation to the word *bliss*, and more so, to the true understanding of what inner peace really is via meditation. Inner peace isn't found watching a documentary on meditation and feeling good afterwards. Inner peace isn't fully realized even during the feeling of understanding we may get when reading a book (such as this) on methods of meditation and the explanations of awakening that follow. They often get us excited for the future of our own practices, but the 'feeling' of inner peace is not the final step as you will come to see.

The only true understanding of bliss and of true peace has and always will be found in a state beyond our own thoughts, and beyond identification with emotions & physical sensations. A true meditative state brought to fruition in personal experience, and the subsequent transcending of it that follows. This too is what meditation reveals. The doorway to our heart. A doorway that leads to a space free of personality or ego. Most importantly it shows us a doorway that if we decide to walk through, delivers us from the stress & suffering, no matter how trivial or devastating, that is brought upon virtually everyone on earth in each day of life. Meditation is in essence, a restart button for the psyche. A 'do-over' so to speak of the ways in which we function as a human being. As a 'me'. And as a 'you'. It provides a chance to wipe the slate clean within our own minds, start fresh cultivating new perspectives on what it means to be here in this physical vessel, and experience the vast range of experiences we witness in each moment, without attaching to it in any way. This is the heart of meditation and the beauty of why such a life-altering practice can be done by anyone, anywhere on Earth, and has been done so for thousands of years. But while this is well known by myself and many others, to those still skeptical I can understand how all that is being said might sound like quite a stretch. Still it's true, the best things in life *are* free. Or at least it is if you ignore the price of this book!

The Essence of Meditation (Why We Meditate)

As will come to be a repetitive theme going forward, the individual experience and what remains once we transcend it is everything in the practice of meditation. Adi Shankarcharya, the short lived yet highly respected 8th Century Indian Philosopher who wrote countless spiritual commentaries would often reference experience as the pillar of meditative practice and spiritual life as a whole, over any amount of knowledge we gain intellectually that contradicts it. One example he would often use was that of what we read (as you are doing at this very moment) versus what we experience externally in the physical world.

Imagine that for countless years you have read dozens of books by multiple religious priests, imams and swamis teaching and preaching that fire is cold. If such was the case and you really never had been in the presence of fire, it would make absolute sense to take the word of these honorable teachers as truth. Without knowing for yourself, and due to your trust in the words of another, you would fully believe that fire was indeed cold and would most likely express this statement as truth to others if the topic of fire arose in conversation. After all, why wouldn't we take the word of a teacher? Surely they can be trusted. And this is true, for the most part. Teachers should be trusted. But the key is not to trust every word uttered with blind faith. This is because if one day down the road we do stumble upon a fire and get close enough to it, we might realize that to our confusion it is not cold! In fact, it is quite the opposite. The fire we now stand in front of is extremely hot! So what do we do now?

Shankarcharya says in this instance that if your experience directly contradicts the words or claims of another, your reality is what you should trust. No matter how many books, teachers, and religions may say that fire is cold, if *you* experience it to be hot, then that experiential truth automatically transcends the alleged truth of others. This is important to understand because we often take the words of others as law, rather than a general guideline we do indeed have the right to stray away from, especially when it comes to meditative practices.

To expand on this, I find the following quote by the late Tibetan Buddhist teacher Chogyam Trungpa relevant, as he once stated in his book *The Truth of Suffering and the Path of Liberation:*

"It is extremely important to persist in our practice without second-guessing ourselves through disappointments, elations, or whatever. In doing so we might actually begin to see the world we carry with us in a more open, refreshing way. Meditation is very much a matter of exercise. Meditation is a working practice."

The key wording here is that of viewing the meditation as working practice indeed. A desk set may come with directions, but you still have to build it. Simply having a manual does not mean the desk will ever build itself. In much the same way, being provided teachings from myself or any other teacher on how to meditate means absolutely nothing without personal effort on your end. And a major part of this personal effort is the ability to intuitively see, from the cracks of true bliss as our practice progresses, what does and doesn't work for each and every one of us. More importantly, it is as Trungpa says, the cultivation of our ability to make minor improvements or changes to these methods without second-guessing ourselves in the process. Trusting your intuition so to speak. And as experience will show us this essence of intuition is nothing more than the True-Self beyond our ego-self, being revealed in meditation.

Sri Ramakrishna often used the parable of the mind & soul being like a candle's flame and the material world acting as the wind. As we well know the flame of a candle is influenced extremely easily by even the slightest gust of wind. So too the human mind is very easily influenced by a multitude of external factors, from the people surrounding us, to where we live, and even things as small as the methods in which we use to meditate.

All these factors are gusts of wind threatening our flame, and if we do not learn to avoid or prevent this wind from rising, it will always cause us to flicker and falter from our natural unmoving state of love and bliss. Therefore, we must utilize the insights gained from going beyond identification so than when we return from our meditative state, adjustments can be made to better deepen our practices on both a material and immaterial level.

This is why we meditate. To harness the ability to discern between the world of material illusions/delusions known as *Maya,* where we are tricked into seeing our attachments as unchangeable, and our problems as everlasting. Instead we can learn to recognize *Maya* as it arises. We begin to see the illusion of time. We become aware that we are not limited beings whatsoever, and that in truth we are much more. You see meditation creates an artist within the mind. In turn it shows us that the art of seeing beyond these illusions is a direct byproduct of allowing ourselves to evolve and live from a space unwavering awareness learned in a deep meditative state. Where one may finally approach each day with true *upekkha* (equanimity) at the core of their actions.

I will admit, the most difficult hurdle of all is the beginning. Yes, in meditation we gain the potential to truly cultivate an ability to live as the True-Self. The eternal Self which is not only infinite, egoless. I may seem to be rambling about all of these endless benefits, for meditation. But the practice truly is endless in its guidance to enable & recognize, as well as overcome the illusions we are tricked into seeing as 'real' at every corner. But also still reminds us to reside in a space of bliss as we spoke of before. For as our awareness expands, so too do our problems contract and shrink. The struggle of allowing this process, while requiring patience and practice to unfold, is one we get to thankfully observe each day as it does. The more we do, the less we judge others and ourselves, and the more we begin to identify as all the souls surrounding us in life too. For as my baba Ram Dass often says in his lessons on identity, a space of pure loving awareness which is what we all are.

As beautiful as the idea of living so purely sounds, much like anything in life, I will again repeat that practice is not just needed, but absolutely necessary in order for such magnificent claims to ever stand the chance of becoming a part of our realities. Especially since it is a space that has trouble existing when our ego-self wants it to. A paradox we will soon address.

It is often expressed in the Hindu philosophy of *Advaita Vedanta* (non-dual teachings of the Veda) which encompass a collection of some of the world's most ancient philosophical teachings and stories from ancient India (also what makes up the foundation of my own spiritual practice) that existence is known as *Brahman*. Brahman is in essence all. Reality, non-reality, even that which extends beyond conception or interpretation. Pure conscious awareness beyond all form. Ultimate Reality on the most fundamental of levels as it is also called quite often. I could go on about this but the point I am trying to make is simply that all of everything, that ever was or ever could be or ever will be, is represented most commonly as *Brahman*. The earth, the solar system, the universe as we know it and even beyond what we currently know is still *Brahman*. Now this might seem irrelevant when learning how to meditate, which is a reasonable assumption to make for those who have yet to experience a true meditative state. Especially if all you care about are the physical and scientific benefits meditation brings. But fear not my friends, that too will be discussed and experienced. The topic of ultimate reality however, is inseparable from such experiences and thus I think talking about it will certainly do good for you.

For simplicities sake if this term seems confusing feel free to apply the term 'universe' or 'God' instead. Whichever your practice prefers. But you see, while all of reality is considered Brahman, we might currently be inclined to see ourselves as separate from the universe. As independent organisms existing within a universe, but not as *the* universe itself, experiencing itself through the vantage of a singular human experiences. One of which that you have deemed, *yours* simply because our consciousness inhabits it. But what meditation serves to teach us, or return us to, is the fundamental and intuitive understanding that we *are* the universe. That this body and all the drama that comes along with living in it belongs to no one. That we always have been, and always will be (regardless of the form we hold) reality itself existing as an endless sea of different forms. This can be seen through the following statement once made by Alan Watts;

"You are something the whole universe is doing
in the same way that a wave is something that the whole ocean is doing."

Referring back to *Advaita* once more, Alan Watts is referring to is our individual nature, being synonymous with all external nature. This is what's known as being a *jivatman*. Living through the experience of being an individual soul (*jiva*) that is experiencing life as a human. And at the same time we are each the *Atman*. A direct reflection of Brahman acting as the individual. In this case, acting as you! Ultimate Reality is what we all are. We are simply blessed, or as some would consider it, cursed with the opportunity to live as if we *aren't* until we rediscover this true nature in the same way that we may see the reflection of the sun in a lake, and easily mistake the reflection of the tree as the actual tree. In this case, seeing our life as nothing but our individual experience, alone in the vastness of reality. It is only when we learn to look up that we see the actual tree in all its glory and recognize the reflection for what it is, an *illusion*.

You are that reflection right now. Unaware of the truth beyond the water, beyond your identity. Only when this perspective of *avidya* (ignorance) we currently hold is eradicated in meditation does one understand the bigger picture. We see that we are not only the reflection but the tree as well.

We see in meditation that the tree and the reflection are one! *Tat Tvam Asi* as it is described in Vedanta. Which means, Thou art that! Atman *is* Brahman. You are the entire universe.

This state of awakening is known as moving from the *jivatman* to *paramatman*, or awakening to the supreme Self... Infinitely here. Consciousness beyond the individual. Pure awareness & love beyond conception or experience.

In the words of Nisargadatta Maharaj,

> "Awareness is primordial; it is the original state. Beginning-less, endless, uncaused, unsupported, without parts, without change... There can be no consciousness without awareness, but there can be awareness without consciousness."

This too is why we meditate. So that we may come to cultivate a practice beyond the need for practice at all! Imagine that! An experience that over time, becomes our daily reality. Only when we move from an experience of peace, to an existence of peace do we truly live as the universe intended... Where the ego-self (which is currently reading this book) stops wanting to *master* or become *good* at the practice of meditation to further fuel its pride. This too can also be recognized as a futile goal that will fade in time, as we travel deeper within ourselves.

The Science of Meditation

While we will all inadvertently attempt to fit whichever method of meditation we decide to follow into our own subjective boxes of understanding, there is also a bright side to the practice which does take place on the material level in regards to the body itself and how it functions.

In my own personal experience, the selling point of meditation was initially for me, (as it is for most of us) the material benefits we may reap from it to strengthen the health of our body and mind. We all want to live with love, and become strong enough mentally to handle any curveball thrown our way. That seeker was me once too. I even remember my first meditation session as a child. For years prior I had chased the rush of drugs and illicit psychoactive compounds to reach new states of internal highs, that allowed me to cope with the many fears I had as a kid. Yet as time progressed my mental health, as well as my body began to lose its strength, and with it my composure. I knew that my sanity was slipping, and that it was time for a change. Searching for natural methods of getting high became my obsession, but out of all the different substances I saw, the suggestion of meditation continued to pop up as a means to increase each compound's effects. This caught my eye. How can sitting still make drugs more powerful? If so does this mean sitting still without drugs provides some sort of powerful experience within the mind as well? And so after some confusing research, I finally sat down to meditate.

What followed was my first dissolution into a true meditative state. I had never felt such overwhelming pleasure and joy! My entire body was vibrating as if I was high. It was at that moment that I realized I was indeed high. High on the reality of what I truly was within. While I fell into a meditative state for roughly 30 minutes, I was most astonished by how I had been so lost in what I would come to understand as cosmic silence, that my body didn't exist until my eyes opened back up, and the physical sensations hit me. It was an experience, that due to the physical effects which followed, convinced me to keep meditating until this day and forever forward. I would later discover that what I had physically experienced was a mixture of Oxytocin and Serotonin that is released within the brain when meditating. An experience you're sure to feel as well.

This combination of compounds allows the mind not only receive a boost of 'good feelings' but also expand our ability to feel, express and understand emotions much more clearly. This experience leads naturally to a feeling of loving awareness that lingers for hours when one finishes their practice and returns to or begins their day. What is more astonishing, recent studies show that by partaking in meditation each day, these results begin to show in as little as one hour after meditation begins, and as late as two weeks after meditation ceases.

Now I'm not here to sell the science of meditation to you. There are many books out there already which successfully do that. But just as reassurance, here is a quick list of scientific benefits to the body and mind that occur as a result of daily meditation.

Meditation increases Immune System function.[1]
Meditation improves the overall health of our heart.[2]
Meditation leads to better problem solving skills.[3]
Meditation reduces stress & anxiety.[4]
Meditation improves our memory.[5]

Now I could continue, but to keep it simple the list of benefits shown under laboratory conditions and in double-blind tests far outweigh the only true argument against meditation, which seems to only be that of not having enough time. But, like anything necessary to a healthy life, from showering to brushing our teeth, we must find room for meditation all the same. In the beginning it will be hard for many, this is no secret. But with time and dedication, we can slowly move beyond the need for instant gratification and revel in the splendor of simply sitting still.

Chapter 2
The Nature of Self

As we will come to notice throughout this manual, many phrases and terms will be used to explain the phenomenal & boundless glory of meditation, as well as the transcendental nature of what it does for us here in this body and on higher levels of being as well. Due to the frequent of following terms, all of which I find to be fully necessary in understanding the heart of meditative practice, I've decided to break them down in order to make this learning process less complicated.

Ego-Self

The Ego-Self is everything we currently think we are or will ever be as an individual. Our roles, including mine as a teacher, student, author and yours as a reader, researcher & seeker. Ego-Self is what creates the individual identity we go by and often worse, believe ourselves to be. This along with our opinions, religions, sexual orientations & any other 'identifier' that we use to express and embrace our own individuality. This is the root cause of why we feel so detached from the planet at large. It is also important to see as well that the ego-self is not an inherently negative or destructive thing. While it is possible to create and live a destructive, dualistic, regressive and close-minded life, it is equally possible, (as is the case with you learning to mediate) to work towards creating an empowering, peaceful, loving and caring ego-self that uses the identity as a tool to improve the world. Taking it seriously, but never too seriously. Still those lost in the ego-self, are virtually always unaware of their soul nature as the whole of reality.

This is the importance of remembering the words such as *identity* and *role* in reference to the ego-self, for it reminds us of what we really are as meditation will show us soon. It helps us play this game called 'life' in a far more relaxed state compared to those who cannot fathom life as a game, or as a temporary experience in an ocean of eternity. But by living vicariously through the ego-self, we truly begin to recognize this *I* as an illusion and that does not permanently exist in any way, shape or form. More so it only exists when we allow it to! This is why so many people take their identity, and the roles of others seriously. At heart they truly believe that they are only their body and their thoughts. This is often a feeling which can become small and claustrophobic. Only after ingesting psychedelic experiences, studying with a Guru, or in our case learning to meditate from a transcendental space can one begin to awaken and realize the actual nature of what we all are.

True-Self (Atman/Brahman)

This is our actual nature. Pure Consciousness, beyond thought. Brahman, as we discovered in detail before, is what the egoless individual awakens too deep within meditative states. Thus we will call it the True-Self moving forward, for it is the only truth. In this state of synchronization with the supreme, our realization is that there is *nothing* but silent conscious awareness that pervades all of reality. Stillness on a level that cannot be expressed nor encapsulated in any linguistic sense, the same way so many souls say events like the birth of a child or the death of a loved one can never be fully described with words.

When we realize the True-Self, which can be expressed most simply by the phrase "I am." We might see this *atman* within as what we are. That I simply am. I am all. I am eternal. I am forever. So on and so forth. One might even transition further into what is considered a *Samadhi* (perfect) state of consciousness or meditation. Here all traces of the ego-self, and the body are completely forgotten, much like they were before our birth into this current human form. However, experiencing these states are always limited. Some lasting fractions of a second, others lasting hours. Which is why the emphasis of meditation is one relying so often on letting go of *any* expectation, and more so letting go of 'getting' anything from it. For benefits will come, that much is given. The True-Self only appears when the Ego-Self has fallen asleep.

When even the highest plane of awakening is temporary, we should thusly see this craving for 'something that will last forever' as a childish wanting bred in ego.

The Soul

If the ego-self is primal, and true self is divinity incarnate, the soul is what lies between with an understanding of these illusory polarities. It is where we should all aim to live from in order to truly make the most out of life. In fact, the entirety of The Vedas, Hinduism's most ancient religious texts state that life is about being aware of our eternal nature, while embracing the ephemeral experience of day to day life in a progressive way. By finding this middle ground we can thusly live through the soul. We embrace the ego-self by using it as a tool to assist us in the material world, but at the same time we must never lose sight of our true interconnectedness with all things.

Living from the soul also helps us navigate the most famous paradox of spiritual practice, which is that awakening always begins in the ego, but ends in the heart. When our path begins, it is the ego-self wanting to meditate, find peace and grow spiritually. But over time we begin to see that there is nothing to achieve and that harmony in life is only a few breaths away. Eventually the ego becomes quiet, allowing the soul to continue on in its place. Surrendering more and more each day to the eternal *Tao*, the way of the universe as it is. Ultimately allowing us the opportunity to surrender into our *dharmic* path which we may follow with utmost compassion for the rest of our lives.

Loving Awareness

While living in the soul, loving awareness is an emotional and mental state of our soul cultivated most often through meditation. It allows us to truly see reality as eternally blissful and subsequently love everything that happens in it. Including every external action/reaction we take part or are witness to as an individual. Loving awareness is to remain forever as the soul while aware of our bodily roles, without slipping completely back into ego-self for too long. An excerpt by my guru Baba Ram Dass explains loving awareness quite clearly;

"Loving awareness is the soul. I am loving awareness. I am aware of everything, I'm aware of my body and my senses and my mind, I'm aware of all of it, but I notice that I'm loving all of it. I'm loving all of the world. The self that I identify with emanates from the ocean of love. The self that is the ego is the ocean of fear. When I am loving awareness I'm aware of everything outside, but pulling into the heart, the spiritual heart, brings me to loving awareness. I'm aware of my thoughts, but loving awareness is simply witnessing them. And loving awareness is in the moment. I have thoughts about the past and future, and those are not helpful, so I dive deep into the present and the presence and in this present moment we will find loving awareness. Only this moment is real, this moment of loving awareness. The past and the future are all just thoughts. In this spiritual heart there is peace, there is contentment, and there is compassion. There is also joy and wisdom, all inside of your spiritual heart and mine. So when you say "I want a peaceful world" you don't look outside, you go inside where peace exists."

Satchitananda (Truth-Consciousness-Bliss)

At this point we understand there is ego-self as unaware of the True Self which is essentially everything. but many still ask just *what* is this everything-ness you speak of? More so, while in meditation how can we decipher these transcendental experiences of extreme bliss and intellectually understand all existence as one occurrence, beyond the illusion of separateness?

The answer is existence itself being *satchitananda*. *Truth, Consciousness, Bliss.*

A word created of three parts simultaneously acting as one: *Sat* (existence), *Chit* (consciousness) and *Ananda* (bliss). Or more simply put, the realization that ultimate reality (*Sat*) is unchanging and unending. Therefore, it can be experienced through the manifestation of consciousness (*Chit*) which appears in the human species lucky for us. Because the unchanging nature of eternity can be experienced, when one awakens to this truth they are filled with supreme bliss (*Ananda*) as a result of understanding it as the nature of this experiential reality. In essence, it is the Atman's experience upon experiencing it is Brahman. All of which occurs in the depths of meditation, that sits peacefully behind all of our thoughts and actions.

Non-Duality

Upon returning from such an experience, or even without knowing it at all yet, we should first embrace this philosophy of oneness as stated earlier in order to see the ultimate goal of meditation.

Which is, according to Nisargadatta Maharaj;

"The primary purpose of meditation is to become conscious of, and familiar with, our inner life (True Self). The ultimate purpose is to reach the source of life and consciousness."

Much like this teacher who preached the philosophy of Advaita, meditation is more than anything, a means o embracing the nature of reality as non-dual. As eternally one. And in my opinion is what will decide if one ever achieves or experiences a successful meditative practice on a deeper level. This includes understand what we are not. For in non-duality there is only oneness without definition. After all, if we know that we are all of it, and allow this knowledge to fuel us. The frightening traits we pick up when living as a lonely individual in the cosmos disappear. Our confidence increases, the anxiety of death and sickness and poverty become less threatening. We begin to see the sacredness of each day in a new light, minute to minute wanting to make the most of it. Embracing Non-duality is embracing all of reality. And there is nothing more empowering than that.

This too means that the themes of separateness from God/ Gods as practiced in some monotheistic & polytheistic religions such as Islam, Catholicism, Rastafari are misleading to say the least. Now don't take that as an attack if you do follow any of these religions. I love you dearly and think, as Sri Ramakrishna once said, "All religions are a path to god/awakening."

What I mean to say is that if we are to live life forever assuming we are separate from God, or from the universe, or even from others people it places the mind in an instinctual state of separating, enacting our survival tactics learned biologically over millions of years of evolution. Such separation breeds competition, especially in a species where survival of the species as a whole is based on fighting to find the right mate, job and friends. In this state we begin to see and think dualistically. A me-versus-them mentality arises. In our case it becomes my mind-versus-meditation. Sadness-versus-peace. Silence-versus-overthinking. As you can see this dualistic state of endless internal competition begins to form subconsciously with every action or thought we have. This is why so many of us seek out meditation in the first place. Because we currently view the world in a highly dualistic sense. A sense that has lead us to suffer dearly.

Therefore, if you don't already understand or follow non-dualism in some sense, I would suggest you begin (at the very least), to at least entertain the understanding of all of reality as one endless &interconnected whole. The same way the clouds are not separate from the sky. For the sky gives rise to the illusion of clouds as individual objects, much like the universe gives rise to our conscious experiences via the human form that most of us too mistake as everlasting.

Chapter 3
How to 'Master'
Meditation

Removing Expectations

My reason for being here isn't to give you anything more than what is necessary. But as we are starting to see, what turns out to be necessary, especially with meditative practice, isn't always a path so clearly illuminated. This lack of direct guidance is one that if not noticed and corrected preemptively, can lead our practice astray very quickly. Primarily due to the ego's obsession with security.

You see at the current moment we as a species simply don't have all the answers we wish we had. The more humanity has evolved, the more we have sought answers from external sources to satisfy the cravings we internally face. At one point the Earth was a flat plane, and then it was discovered to be a sphere at the alleged center of all reality. After this we realized that the Earth was actually just one of nine, and now eight planets orbiting the sun. And for the first time we were faced with the truth of our reality not being the center of all creation. As time passed we discovered more suns. Billions of them! Many with their own planetary systems existing hundreds of millions of miles away.

But as far as we knew, the Milky Way galaxy we existed within was the only galaxy in all of existence. In fact, it was the whole of existence.

However, just a short while later we figured out that not only did other galaxies exist, but in actuality billions of galaxies exist too as far as the eye can see! Even as far as infra-red & x-ray cameras could see it was proven that the physical reality we inhabit isn't consolidated, but instead is looking more and more to be a seemingly infinite expanse of space. This is a concept the vast majority of us still can't currently wrap our minds. Although we have developed the ability to discover new and complex truths about the material universe in which we live, we are far from accepting it as a species on a conceptual level.

And so we suffer. The more we learn, the more questions we have, and the more we recognize just how many of these questions will never be answered in our lifetime, and the more we dive into a destructive cycle of perceived pointlessness in existence as a whole. You see we are a species of endless expectations. We expected the Earth to be flat. We expected the earth to be the center of all reality and we expected this galaxy to be the only galaxy. So of course currently expect ourselves to be real entities. With real problems and real passions.

So why do we do this when time and time again our insignificance among the vastness of the cosmos seems to be continually proven? Well, we can thank this method of thinking to the never-ending quest for absolute clarity and security the ego-self is searching for. Which is also reason you picked up this book. You may be facing mental insecurities, emotional weaknesses, major shifts in life and simply wanted to deepen your spiritual practice. In doing this you naturally saw meditation as a secure solution. "If I can control/quiet my mind I will be better."

And so we enter into these pages with the expectation of mastering meditation and often with an ideal image in our head of us sitting in a serene space of clarity weeks from now, impervious to the outside world, the way we see meditative masters and monks in images from books and documentaries we watch. This is the ego-self building a platform of expectations for the meditative practice. It is already assuming it will love meditation, and furthermore be a 'successful meditator when:

1.)   We aren't sure if we'll like the meditative methods to follow at all.

2.) The entire concept of a 'successful meditator' is an oxymoron.

This is same way it would be if you considered yourself a 'compassionate killer'... So we must ask ourselves, if the inevitable fruit of meditation is awakening into a space of love beyond personality and identity as a whole, then *who* would it be recognizing itself as a great or successful meditator? *Who* would take pride in such an occurrence? Furthermore, when returning from a meditative state will someone be there to fuel our ego with 'great job' and 'wow this feels great'? If so, we must recognize that this is none other than our ego-self making such comments, trying to infiltrate our practice.

I raise this awareness of looking out for one's own ego as meditation begins and progresses so that the main message of this book can shine through. A truth not often expressed;

You are already a master of meditation. Indeed, I will say you have already mastered the practice of meditation! You, in all reality, don't even need this book due to how natural the meditative practice is to you! So how come you are here? Expectations.

Our *dharma* (true path in life), will always lead us where we need to go so long as we make the effort to follow it purely. You are here following your path, and that path is one which included meditation. However, we in the West often chalk experiences up to free will, rather than our *karma* (actions we take in each moment) resulting in where we are now. Because of this continuity is lost. We fail to see the continuation of our path in every moment and instead see each situation as separate from the one before. This leads us into expecting and attempting to predict or decide what will come next, even when it may be out of our hands. So how do we overcome this and why might it matter?

The trick is to live in the moment, aware of how the past has lead us here, but excited for the potential that the future may hold.

In doing so we not only vanquish suffering, but remove the destructive practice of expectancy from our lives altogether. Including its removal from that of meditation. Allow me to provide an example that I often use with my students:

Suppose you meet someone at a coffee shop who peaks your interest. You work up the courage to ask him/her to dinner and to your delight they say yes. Although we may be ecstatic in that moment, it quickly fades and hours later as we head out the door to dinner we might find ourselves full of nervousness and fear for the meal.

"What if I say something wrong?" "What if they don't like me?" "How do I explain my job/hobbies the right way?" So on and so forth.

You see, as I referenced earlier the ego prefers boring security to questionable excitement. Even after exciting things happen, such as someone agreeing to go on a date with us, (or in the case of this book experiencing a transcendental meditative state) once the initial excitement fades we return to a seeking of security instead of the momentary experience. In doing so we subconsciously begin to set expectations for others (our date in this case) and for ourselves. Low and behold, it might end up ruining the night completely if our over-thinking doesn't subside. I myself have overthought and set expectations unnecessarily on many occasions that have in turn, created problems. So how do we go about fixing this dilemma we will certainly face?

The key rests with your ability to accept all realities simultaneously. What this means is that as we prepare for the upcoming date, recognize when your expectations are beginning to arise. Instead of fueling them however, begin to accept them as truths on both ends of the spectrum. We must tell ourselves, "I accept that this date will lead nowhere." And at the same time we follow up this affirmation by saying, "I also accept that this date will lead to a long and happy relationship for life." After stating both simply sit for a minute and truly in your heart accept them as equally true. In doing this, you will soon notice that your expectations cease to exist! After all, how can expectations arise if we are consciously accepting each potential reality that might play out as true? The beauty is that it *can't*. This is what it means to be a master of meditation. And this can be achieved, or more so realized, the moment we remove our attachment to the benefits we wish to gain. This method of thinking will continue on into waking life as well. The hobbies we currently partake in, the way we raise our children, there is an endless sea of possible factors that seem to separate us from meditative mastery, all we must to is acknowledge them and move on.

I won't lie and say that meditation *can,* in any way it is presented (be in this book or another), guarantee with complete certainty that you will 'get it', and begin to awaken, or let go of these dualistic thoughts. But I can say with utmost certainty it will very much increase the likelihood of this happening, as well as solving the issues we currently face in our current ego-roles more so than virtually anything else will. So *must* embrace the illusory polarities meditation seems to hold above. At least until we learn to see through our dualistic modes of thinking. This can be done simply by,

1.) Embracing that we are nothing.

We embrace that we are nothing in particular, and that there certainly is a possibility that we cannot in this lifetime meditate successfully whatsoever. No matter how hard we try.

2.) Simultaneously accepting that we are everything.

That we are eternally powerful and unending masters of meditation. And that nothing can stop us from awakening the transcendent state of love and bliss that is our true nature when we sit and close our eyes today, tomorrow and forever forward. Heck you might even write your own book on the topic one day!

You see when both are realized as equally true scenarios, the polarities cancel each other out and we are left with nothing but the direct experience of this moment. An experience free of expectations and ego, which in turn allows the practice of meditation to finally occur as it had always been intended to. Beyond identity, beyond pride and beyond titles. Sitting down not as anything in particular, just as pure awareness watching a body breathe.

The 'Right' Way to Breathe

As with any physical task, it remains important that we drill the basics into our mind before moving on to the next step. In the case of meditation, our aim is to balance our awareness on of either a single point of focus, from the movement of our breath, to a mantra/single word. Or it is to allow our mind to go completely blank and just flow without grasping at any form. Even thoughts. However, getting to this state of actual practice can be easily inhibited if our breathing is occurring unnaturally as well.

For example, if someone were to hand you a pencil and ask you to draw a square, those of us with experience writing could easily draw one in a matter of seconds due to our familiarity with how to hold the pencil. But for those who have never held a pencil, they might find themselves holding it the wrong way. Doing so could then easily create a noticeable difficulty with drawing what is supposed to be a simple shape and simple task to others. This too occurs if the process of breathing. A task so simple our body does it involuntarily virtually all of the time. We are simply not used to controlling it 24/7 and so when we finally sit with it, it becomes a subject of hyper-focus by the mind during our journey inward. The ancient Sufi scholar Rumi illustrates this point beautifully in one of his late poems;

"There is one way of breathing that is shameful and constricted.
Then there's another way; a breath of love that takes you all the way to infinity."

In this sense the incorrect and correct ways of breathing are extremely simple to differentiate. If you can do this, it will allow your focus to remain in a space of purity, rather than a space of worry or over-analysis. Often I have seen teachers advise the student to count their breath. "Three second inhale, hold for two seconds, three second exhale." Etc…. In other cases, I have heard some suggest students to fill their lungs as fully as possible, and only then to begin to exhale. Some even go as far as to say that in breathing one should try to measure the breath so that it is 'even'. All of this, at least in my experience, is advice that should be cast out completely when learning to meditate.

The problem with making a task of breathing is just that, adding an unnecessary task to our practice! We are now not meditating, but instead sitting and counting and measuring our breath *and* simultaneously attempting to clear our mind! This quite clearly cannot be done all at once. After all, I can't hold my hands together and clap them at the same time. Can you? Probably not. Can anyone? Again probably not. So what are we to do then about our breath? Absolutely Nothing.

You see, much like the heart and our eyelids, breathing is something the body does on its own unless we try controlling it. Thankfully though if we surrender this need for forced control we do not drop dead! Instead the body picks right back up where it started and regulates the breath on its own. This primal instinct of the body is actually of massive benefit to the mind and subsequently to our soul, for it means all we must do to breathe 'correctly' is relinquish control of the breath completely. Instead of trying to focus on a mantra and your breath, simply focus on the mantra! Allow the body to breathe at its natural pace and in doing so there is one less hurdle for us to overcome.

For months I tried to breathe in a way I thought was 'balanced' and 'proper' but to no avail. I couldn't find a way to make my controlled breathing constant while sitting according to lessons I had learned online. It wasn't until I visited a local temple and spoke with a Swami directly that I was advised against attempting to dominate my own breath, and instead to just practice the task of surrendering to the body while I sat. Allowing the physical organism through which we experience life to regulate the breath on its own. Only when I finally did begin to surrender to the natural process of breathing did my practice begin to truly deepen in a way it never had before when the subconscious focus of control was still active in my mind.

I should also add that while mindful breathing is an amazing tool as a way to focus internally while we are out and about in the world, it is best left for the active experience of wakeful spiritual practice. Since we will all be sitting or resting on the floor with our intention situated in pure love, it is better we give up the control we think we need to hold over ourselves. This allows the body to guide itself in order to truly awaken the soul in a way it simply cannot while the ego seeks to control an aspect of the identity we still cling to when attempting to override the body. This leaves us open to simply observe reality, as soul nature incarnate. As all that we are during the process of this body breathing. Rising. Falling. Rising. Falling. Easy as that.

I will include though that prior to sitting in meditation, and allowing the breath to flow freely that if we do wish to control the breath before releasing it, the practice of *pranayama* (breath controlling exercise) can be applied. This practice can be done before any of the methods to come in this book and is an amazing tool for activating the PNS, or parasympathetic nervous system which in turn relieves anxiety and relaxes the body which when sitting to meditate might still be agitated from whatever might have transpired leading up to this moment. For more on pranayama & it's methods I recommend you read *Light on Pranayama* by the yoga master B.K.S Iyengar.

Impatience: The Hidden Poison

Once breathing becomes second nature, our practice will also begin to exponentially deepen with each meditative session we sit in... Or so our ego may think. But just because we are now learning to live in the moment fully, and to allow the material body to act on its own, should never lead us down the path of assuming our meditation will equally reflect the changes we notice. In essence, just because we master one skill, doesn't mean we will master another in the same amount of time. The soul has no calendar for when awakening will happen. The ego might, but the True-Self has no agenda one way or the other. Both awakening and non-awakening are fine when we sit beyond our roles, because we will in such states recognize that we are always exactly where we need to be. Yet, we rarely see that getting where we need to be and being where we *want* to be are often oceans apart.

When I visited temples at a younger age I did so out of an increasing level of impatience building up within my mind. Endless accounts from guided practices and highly regarded books had convinced me that if all the directions listed were duplicated that the perfection of my own meditative practices would come quickly. But after months of struggles I grew evermore restless and agitated. Although visiting the temple did in some ways solve the issues I had been facing, upon reflection I couldn't help but realize just how wasteful and selfish my façade of a practice had become in the months leading up to my Swami's intervention. You see, when we allow impatience to grow within, the mind seeks out new means of conscious focus so that it can distance itself from that which it cannot have. In the case of meditative practice (as I personally witnessed), impatience is a silent killer because it alters the entire foundation of what our practice is.

Instead of sitting to let go of the identity and awaken loving awareness, the impatience boiling within seeks out new practices as a means to overcome the issue it is currently facing. No longer do we find ourselves meditating, instead we find ourselves sitting, and attempting to (in this case) defeat the problem of controlling our breath, or of awakening. No longer do we sit simply to sit, instead impatience will secretly lead us down a path of sitting as a competition to how well and fast I can clear my mind. How frequently I can meditate more than 20 minutes. Judging how physically good this session felt in comparison to the last and so forth. When impatience is not recognized it will derail the entirety of our practice completely without us ever becoming aware that it had done so, as was the case for me.

In this understanding of impatience, the solution, (much like surrendering to the breath) is equally simple. We merely need to surrender to the practice itself as it exists right *now*. This is because impatience ceases to exist if we forgo our attachments to the past or future completely. After all, it is a state of the mind that can only exist in the realm of time. So if we are living, and more importantly meditating in the present moment, it truly has no ability to impact the mind whatsoever. All we must do as we sit down to practice is to embrace this moment.

Do not sit down and think about last week's meditation session. Do not begin to breathe and wonder if next week you'll be sitting in a better posture. Remove the concept of time completely from your mind, and you will transcend the hold it so easily has over those of us without a consistent meditative practice. Pure bliss is timeless. Cosmic consciousness is timeless. Love is timeless. So too should our practice be.

Reliance: The Ego's Crutch

While the benefits of meditation far outweigh any perceivable consequences that spring up from the mistakes we are here now correcting, reliance is often the hardest to recognize. Why, you might ask? Primarily due to enjoyment. Much like a drug releases chemicals within the mind that elicit a positive response, so too does meditation as discussed before. The problem with such an effect is that some become reliant on their practice, either for the rush it gives them, or they find one method works more easily than the rest and never want to let it go. A reasonable response to have, but still one we should remain cautious of as our practice deepens, for the mind has a tendency to mold into any shape, the way water will always mold to the shape of the container surrounding it.

Thankfully, all we must do to avoid becoming reliant upon our practice is to write down the following message to ourselves every few days, and sit with each question until we can answer it honestly.

1.) Am I identifying with my practice?

This question helps to constantly remind us of our true nature. That we are not a 'meditator', and that we should not seek such a title in any form. I may teach meditation, and when asked what I do, might refer to the title of teaching it, however I don't associate this title or this practice as that which makes up the essence of 'me' defining my conscious organism. By constantly asking ourselves if identification has slipped through the cracks, we gain the ability of witnessing the practice from a loving, but detached vantage. In doing so we can practice constantly without the ego becoming reliant on using meditation as a secret method of self-validation and pride.

2.) Why am I using this method of meditation?

One of the reasons I included multiple ways of meditation in this manual wasn't to complicate the practice, or to create a competition between the differences the methods to come. The purpose of multiple mechanisms for the mind, body & soul is so we can remain open to them all, instead of picking one and becoming isolated within it. We must lovingly ask ourselves why it is we are using the method we use. For virtually all of us the answer may seem the same, "Well, because it works the best.". By answering this question, it forces our mind to refresh, like a webpage on the internet, and with it new answers or shifts in perspective may arise. We may recognize that by 'working' we mean it is giving us the best 'feel-good' response. Knowing this, we might remember that the 'feel-good' aspect of meditation is only the surface of its complex and deep purpose as a whole, and thusly switch to a method that provides less physical stimuli, and more space to dive within. Another example is that we might subconsciously decide to use, is a method that goes along with our religious or spiritual practices too, instead of picking up the meditation that may intuitively work better.

In the case of this book, when asking friends which method they preferred prior to practicing, many Hindu friends instantly decided upon Mantra Meditation, while many of my Buddhist family quickly stood on the side of Insight Meditation. This is quite a hyperbolic conclusion for me to come to but still, this could easily occur for any number of us. By asking ourselves with true love in mind, just *why* we are using the method we do, we can easily bypass the ego's preferred answer and access the root of truth behind our decision. In doing this we again dispel the reliance of one method forever, and allow the soul to openly practice many different methods (if needed). The same way we often notice many Gurus and spiritual teachers utilizing the teachings of multiple religions and cultures, instead of being confined to a single one.

3.) If my practice changed, or stopped, how would I handle this shift?

This final question, in regards to overcoming reliance on our practice, is that of hypothetically asking ourselves what can be seen in some ways, threatening. What if my practice ended? What if I couldn't do it? Above all, how would I react? As with anything that provides us assistance in life, humans very quickly and very easily react with volatility the moment it is hidden or removed from their hands, or in this case our minds. For instance, we might all have a favorite morning cereal, or a favorite song we listen to over and over again. Still, most of us understand that from time to time we open the pantry only to find an empty cereal box, or find ourselves without our phones, and thusly without access to our favorite song. While we may have attachments to these items in a sense, we are also accepting of the times it is not present in our life. We must treat meditation the same.

If we become reliant on meditation, what will we do when we wake up late and realize we don't have time for our usual morning session? What if our nightly practice is thwarted by construction taking place across the road? Will we allow our ego-self to throw a fit and complain within that we aren't getting what we want? Or will we take the advice of the practice itself and instead, see the beauty of change and the beauty of allowing the play of life to throw curve balls our way. This is why questioning a change in our practice is pivotal to defeating any hidden reliance upon meditation that can secretly grow within. For as we have already established, all the ego seeks is comfort and solidity in life. The soul instead allows life to be. No need to interrupt, no need attempting to override that which exists out of our control.

If you ask yourself this question and notice that you get upset, or that you would have trouble dealing with such a shift, then in your next session focus on detachment. Focus on the fragility and temporal nature of life as we experience it! In doing this our practice grows, our ego shrinks, and we begin to flow as the waves do in the ocean. Without agenda, without expectation and above all without a reliance on the wave behind it, or the storm brewing overhead.

Modes of Sitting

As we move on from these lessons to avoid the pitfalls and interruptions of meditation, we should quickly discuss posture and sitting. Much like breathing, sitting, (depending on who you are learning from, where you are learning, and how the teacher was taught) will be the reason why you sit the way you do. But in truth, you may sit any way you please! For there are a variety of postures for the body to hold in meditation, with our hands in a variety of spiritually interactive positions, commonly known as *mudras*. So, which is right? Again, whichever works best for you.

While Zazen has its own sitting posture that differs from Vipassana, the truth of the matter is that for us entering the practice for the first time, much like trying too hard to control our breath, we do not want to fall out of a meditative state or stop ourselves from ever entering into one simply because we are too worried about the logistics or meaning of how we are sitting. Many devout practitioners may vehemently disagree with what I am saying here, but I believe this is only due in part to how they were taught to follow their practice, the same way a devoutly religious person has no room for accepting the ideals of another religion. There is no harm here, but at most basic level, the more comfortable we are, the easier we will find ourselves falling into a state of blissful awareness.

Personally, I sit in Zazen posture. This means I sit on a *zafu,* or a small round cushion that rests upon a bamboo *zabuton.* Which is a large soft mat used to provide comfort to the knees and feet. In doing so the ability to sit in a correct posture, with a straight, aligned spine, becomes much easier than when attempting to sit cross legged flat on the ground. My hands rest in my lap in what is known as a *Burmese Position* where the left hand rests facing upward upon the right hand, with the thumbs meeting above them and touching ever so slightly. Imagine making a small "O" with your hand in your lap. This is what the mudra looks like. Again however, this is merely the position that works for me. Do not use my method simply because it is the one I use. Research the various postures of sitting on your own time. *Full Lotus, Half Lotus, Burmese, Seiza!* The list goes on my friend! It is up to you to try them out and discover which one provides not only the best postural position, but simultaneously the most comfort and least distractions.

Can we lay flat on the ground or on a bed when we meditate? Yes. Can we use a back rest or utilize a wall in our room to help with posture? Again, yes you can. Find what works the best for you, and what allows you to truly embrace silence free of distraction, and that will be the correct method of sitting for you in regards to meditation.

The Nature of Silence

A highly respected and well versed meditation teacher known as Adyashanti speaks quite often on the essence and importance of silence in regards to meditation. Not in the sense of the room or area in which we are being completely silent, but instead he expresses the notion of mental silence in meditation as the penultimate factor to our own inner awakening process. On one occasion he went on to state the following;

"All that is necessary to awaken to yourself as the radiant emptiness
of spirit is to stop seeking something more or better or different,
and to turn your attention inward to the awake silence that you are."

Often we think of words like emptiness in regards to the self as negative. We don't want to be empty, for that means the ego-self in which we take such pride must be gone! Similarly, he speaks about awakening the silence that we are. Awakening silence...

Quite a paradoxical combination of words, in the same way that saying something like 'sleeping awake-ness' might not initially seem to make sense. But at this moment that is exactly what we are. We are awake in the sense of ego and in the sense of associating life and existence to that of this human body. But we are simultaneously asleep in the spiritual sense and in the sense of knowing the truth of what we are beyond the roles we play. So when we meditate we must always remember (even if we aren't fully in sync with it yet), that we are indeed at our core pure, silent, conscious awareness. No voice. No personality. No reaction. Simply awareness.

And as such we will come to see as we sit in silence, free from thoughts, that awareness *is* silence! Therefore, when meditating always remember silence as the natural state and thusly allow your mind to flow freely until the waters still, and silence fills us. We may chant a word, we may focus our mind on a feeling, but in this space of *dhyana*, or a single point of focus within the mind, we must allow the mind the freedom to silence itself. If it begins to still and let go of the word, let it. If the mantra's repetition is assisting the silence, keep chanting! We mustn't think or focus on how many times a word or saying is chanted, nor should we try to limit the silence in which we are to the time frame we have for our meditation session either.

Above all the methods to follow and the awakening meditation holds the ability to provide across all religions, cultures and eras is that of transcending the personal self, and awakening into a space oneness. Allowing the pure conscious nature of what we are, the inner atman, to synchronize with all of reality in this moment. A moment that is eternally silent and simultaneously blissful.

Freedom from Thoughts

Silence may sound like quite the experience to surrender into, however we must not forget that in order to do so we must traverse the seemingly endless sea of thoughts we house within our minds. In the movie *Finding Nemo* there is a scene where the main character, a high maintenance clown-fish, accidentally wanders into a massive group of very poisonous jellyfish. In doing so he becomes instantly afraid, and begins to dart around the jellyfish desperately seeking an escape route back to the safety of the open ocean, with no logic at all. When we begin to practice meditation, and even at this very moment in our lives a great many of us consider ourselves victims to our own thoughts lost in a sea of them. Swami Vivekananda, a disciple of the Saint Sri Ramakrishna, was a very devout advocate of just how strong the power of thoughts, and how we identify with them can impact us when he said the following in the 20th century;

"We are what our thoughts have made us; so take care about what you think. Words are secondary. Thoughts live; they travel far."

I bring this up because it is imperative if we don't already know, that what we think has the power not just to liberate us from suffering and lead one in full control of his mind into a state of enlightenment, but also on the opposite end of the spectrum it can very easily lead us into a downward spiral of chaos and insurmountable depression. In meditation our thoughts will most likely fall into one of these two categories, and like the fish above, we can very often overreact and get lost in such thoughts. The problem with this is that when we do so, we often see it as a mistake and subconsciously chastise ourselves for thinking. So we go from thinking, to thinking about how bad it is we are thinking! If this continues we may find ourselves thinking about how thinking makes us feel bad about thinking!

Do you see here just how complicated and corrosive being lost can seem during meditation? No matter how good or bad the thought may be, the key to freeing ourselves from them and escaping, as the clown-fish finally escaped the hordes of jellyfish, is to detach ourselves from them completely. As we sit, instead of seeing each thought as 'my thought', simply shift your perspective farther away to the witness within and instead recognize it as 'a thought'. No ownership involved, no identity to claim it as theirs. The power in loving detachment from our thoughts is that since it is no longer ours, we hold no emotional connection to it! And the better we get at doing this, the less of an emotional influence it will have on us.

In this space of simply *witnessing* the thoughts arise and disappear, we will receive for the first time a look at how our conscious mind comes to exist. We will no longer think of it as a rigid thing, but as an endless sea of change. And doing this alone (while it may work), can still leave room for us to again forget to remain in the witness or the objective space of love beyond thoughts. Therefore, while implementing this separateness of the eternal-self and temporal thoughts, the more we simplify it the easier it becomes to truly see that we are indeed more than the mind. So when a thought does arise, simply refer to it as such! When an emotion arises, simply refer to it as such and we will almost instantly snap back into oneness, instead of mulling over the mind's clutter and slowly trying to reinforce to ourselves that we are separate.

Say we are sitting down, having just began our meditation a few minutes earlier and already we find ourselves wondering what we will eat for dinner tonight. We could easily stop and say, "Oh, here is another thought arising. I am not this thought, let me return to silence." Yet this is sixteen words. Two full sentences, each of which take us out of the moment. So how do we simplify this loving detachment even more? Isolate what is happening to one single word. In this case, when we notice that we are in our identity thinking about breakfast, simply isolate it for what it is, a thought, and say in your mind, "Thoughts." Before returning to the breath.

Similarly, if we feel the sensation of sadness or excitement within us. Don't try to run from it or ignore it. This will only prolong out attachment to said feelings because by doing this, we are identifying with it as a feeling we 'need' to get away from. This need is nothing but attachment to ego-self, and as the core tenants of Buddhism state, attachment is the root cause of suffering. And so when we do feel these emotions or any other arise, much like our thoughts we can simply acknowledge it as a temporary process of our illusory identity, say quietly or silently; "Sadness" or "Excitement" and move on.

This subconsciously frees us because it functions as an internal affirmation, while also being an instant reminder that *we are not* these thoughts or emotions. Not in meditation, and not when we go about our daily life either. We are the eternal manifesting into a singular vantage just to experience the illusion of a limited self that is all! In doing so we allow the true Self within to move on from said thoughts and emotions as soon as they arise. No judgement, no guilt, no worries, no expectations and most importantly no identification with what they are, where they will go or what they might mean to our identities! Thoughts will arise. This is an inescapable fact of life and how we currently live it.

So long as we allow them to be just that, and not something that is influencing or effecting us, the meditative state will flow through us like the raging waters of a river following the downpour of rain.

Meditation Commonalities in this Manual

While each of these methods to come are in many ways unrelated and completely unique, there are also a few common denominators between them. They are listed here so that they do not clutter or add unnecessary steps for the teachings to come.

1.)   The ideal time for these meditation practices are either in the early morning or right before bed.

2.)   Wherever you meditate, attempt to do so in an area with a great amount of silence, except for the Scanning Meditation. In this case a slightly noisy area is ideal.

3.) Sit however suits you best! A common posture would be in a half lotus, with our hands sitting in our lap, or resting on our knees in the mudra you prefer. Just find one that feels right!

4.) While sitting, the head should be slightly tilted to face the ground, but not looking straight down. A great indicator is our line of sight ending about three feet in front of us if our eyes were to be open.

5.) Stretch before beginning. This is so the body can be less reactive during extended periods of sitting. The less focus on pain, the easier we can return to intense isolated awareness.

6.) Try not to use an alarm! Meditation when ended abruptly can easily hurt what progress we have made while in a meditative state due to the abrasive nature of most alarms.

7.) If using an alarm, use one with very soft sounds. Preferably running water, trees in the wind, and so forth.

Chapter 4
Insight Meditation

For most of us, less means more when regarding meditation. Yet for others knowledge can often deepen not only our resolve, but our truth in the practice itself. If after reading you find yourself wanting more than just the steps provided, I urge you to follow your heart and seek out more wisdom in regards to these ancient and effective practices. In the case of *Vipassana* or Insight Meditation, the history of its impact on the world could fill an entire book on its own with room for a second. Why? Because insight meditation is arguably the most popular mode of awakening there is when presented to someone who has never before picked up the practice of meditation. Vipassana itself roughly translated from Sanskrit to 'seeing through' or 'seeing clearly' as is the case with insight as a whole. For those of us unfamiliar, insight is one's ability to cultivate a comprehensive and true to form understanding. In the case of meditation this means insight into both the true nature of reality itself as we spoke of earlier, as well as attempting to show us that in doing so the suffering we face while living out our roles can also be resolved.

This is what makes Insight meditation in the form of Vipassana such a powerful tool, it not only shows us the universal truth, but allows us to return to daily life and subsequently live out our days when not meditating, free of suffering completely. All accomplished by simply watching the breath as it rises and falls, without identifying with it.

When this happens we may then return from this deep meditative state and apply such awakenings to bettering our lives, and the lives of those around us. In actuality is often said by Buddhist scholars that Vipassana itself is not the meditation. While mindfulness and insight are involved in this mode of meditation, Vipassana is seen as a mental attribute we cultivate. For such clear sight includes the ability to see beyond delusions that exists not just in the mind, but physically as well.

The formula to correctly practicing Vipassana is first to recognize which aspects or influences will guide us to allowing insight to manifest while meditating. According to the *Dhammapada*, the world's most highly regarded collection of Buddhist teachings, these are the aspects of Vipassana that allow it to function. By integrating them correctly, anyone can successfully meditate using the Insight method within a few short days. However, I will say that this is a mixture of modern insight, mixed with the layout of traditional Vipassana practice originated by Goenka himself. I do this out of respect to the true lineage Vipassana holds. Part of which means that before teaching the true, unaltered methods of Vipassana, one should attend multiple ten day silent retreats at one of their many centers. Now this is something the vast majority of us don't have the time to do, and I am currently one of these individuals. So some Vipassana

Masters say that without experiencing a ten day silent retreat, one cannot fully practice Vipassana, no matter how sporadically they do it. And although I respectfully disagree, I honor their tradition will thusly present a slightly modified yet fully effective method of Insight.

How to Practice Insight Meditation

1.)   **Begin by finding a quiet, peaceful place to sit.** This can be done alone in our room, at a public park or at the end of a yoga class with friends. So long as the external distractions are kept to minimum all will be fine.

2.)   **Sit or lay down and find a position that can last the length of your entire meditation session.** In essence once we find a working position, it is important that one does not move. This is so distractions can be minimized, non-meditative habits (such as repositioning our body constantly) do not become common place. Our body is adaptive. The more we stick with a working position, the less we will notice it.

3.)   **Take 3 deep breaths.** Inhale deeply through the nostrils, and exhale through the mouth. With each inhale remind yourself that you are the universe, with each exhale we are letting go of any stress present in the body.

4.)   **Close the eyes, but do not force them to close.** Allow them to stay as closed as they naturally can without attempting to control them.

5.)   **Allow awareness to situate in silence.** As Vipassana is a practice of allowing insights to arise from within focus on anything direct, even the breath has the potential to hinder this from occurring. Although some methods of Vipassana disagree, this is personally what I have found to be true and most effective. So in order to allow these insights to occur, one must practice the first of the three main aspects of Vipassana, starting with our breath.

Awareness of the Moment & Breath

Being in the now might seem like a given in regards to meditation, but for many of us as mentioned earlier an endless array of factors can easily throw us off. Therefore, both Vipassana and more modern Insight methods such as this request we simply *return to silent awareness*, in this case that of pure consciousness. Silence beyond personality or ego. This is so that each time we begin trailing off to follow a thought or feel an emotion, or if we have just forgotten the breath at all we can see that all of these 'experiences' only happen when witnessed through our personalities. So when you see this, just drop the role and return to silence! That's all you must do! Let what arises rise, and in the same breath as it leaves, watch it leave. We are not here to focus on any 'thing' when sitting with moment, instead our focus in the moment should be that of merely being a spectator to existence. Letting it all play out on its own accord.

6.)   **Return to this silence when thoughts arise.** At this point we are sitting with all of reality. The rising and the falling of the breath continues to flow as we sit behind it, watching it as such without conception. While we do this always remember to simply *be* that transcendental silence if anything comes to mind. Allowing the breath to just *be* as well. Make sure not to mistake yourself as the 'watcher' of the breath, or the 'achiever' of silence. Just breathe and be as it happens naturally. Nothing more.

Clarity of Mind

In this this phase of step six, those familiar with Insight practice most likely begin to have flashes of understanding or insights into our true nature. However, for the vast majority of us going directly from silent observation to absolute understanding this will take practice. This practice is that of bypassing the thoughts which will arise and attempt to steer us away from awareness. This is when the second major tool of insightful practice: that of *acute mental clarity* in regards to our thoughts. What this means is to catch and subsequently release our thoughts when they occur. Vipassana practice advises we catch them before they begin to distract us too much. Once we have recognized that a thought has occurred, we then remind ourselves that it is a product of the ego, an illusion of the mind. When this is done we release it from focus and let the mind go blank. All of which can be done in a matter of seconds as our practice deepens.

7.) **As insights begin to manifest within, allow them to fully form before interacting.** In doing so we will begin to notice over time these intuitive yet powerful insights arise from what seems to be nowhere and fill us with an absolutely supreme understanding of our true nature and of peace.

8.) **Remember not to cling to the insights which arise.** The power of insight meditation comes through the temporal clarity it provides to us. Sort of like a spark of divine light in the darkness. These awakenings we are endowed with as meditate fill us, are those of transcendental understandings and will just as quickly fade away. Much like smoke, although we may think it has a definitive shape, but the moment we attempt to grab it, it slips away forever. This too applies when the mind becomes clear of identity. For the insights only arise beyond ego. If the ego tries to snap back into control and grasp these insights for themselves, you will notice they disappear instantly. Instead of doing this, which in the beginning I promise you will catch yourself attempting to do, just let the soul sit in peace. The eternal self, in time, will come to know these insights as truth. Life as temporary. Existence as bliss. The longer we sit in this meditation the quicker these concepts become unshakable realities in our heart.

9.) **Thank the universe, then open your eyes.** After sitting in this blissful space, when we feel ready in our heart we may take one last deep breath in through the nose, letting love fill us in the process. Once this is done slowly open our eyes and welcome back the world with love.

10.) **Remain with this gratitude.** Eyes now open, hold in your heart a deep feeling of gratitude not only for what you just experienced and learned, but for all living organisms on the earth as well. Hold this in mind as you return to your life and go about your day.

With this, we have completed our first sessions of Insight Meditation. We are from this point forward increasing not just our own inner peace, but the ability we house to intuitively understand life for what it really is, and to love it unconditionally as such. The longer we practice, the more we will feel this love for the world as a whole begin to radiate from within. Day by day the love and the lessons insight meditation provide to us will awaken the true Self and allow it to flourish unconditionally. Insight at this point will no longer be a tool for attaining peace, but instead will often become a direct channel for our own personal connection with the universe. As time continues, one will begin to notice (according the the *Pali Canon* of Theravada Buddhism) that our initial attachments to the major hindrances of material life that keep us from living in bliss begin to fade away. Sensual desires fade as we find the truth within, our repressed anger and grudges disappear as we begin to see all as a reflection of the whole. Even the heavy mentalities of sadness and depression that many of us carry around due to the way we live now (seeing these thoughts as ultimate truths when they are in actuality relative) lighten as the heart awakens and bliss fills us. Essentially, the clutter that we carry in our mind keeps us living in either the past or the future, missing out on the beauty of this moment. This ends with insight. Most importantly, any doubts we hold either consciously or subconsciously about ourselves end here as well.

Our meditation practice and even what will happen next week are lost as we begin to see that so long as we are here, all becomes clear and allows us to truly prepare for any reality that may arise. For as it is stated in *A Course in Miracles*,

> "Nothing real can be threatened.
> Nothing unreal exists.
> Herein lies peace."

Chapter 5
Mindfulness
Meditation

While Vipassana is a practice with quite a few steps and philosophies rooted in classical Buddhist schools, another method known as Mindfulness Meditation is what many consider the quintessential method of meditation due to its singular step which encompasses the entire practice. Also while Vipassana looks within (which can be difficult for those of us who have never truly sought answers this way), Mindfulness instead centers around the focus of our awareness being external. The body and the sensory inputs we receive from its surroundings encompass the majority of what this practice will direct our attention towards.

In the case of mental health, Mindfulness is much more suited for those of us who seem to have endless amounts of energy, both physical and mental, as it is completely allowing of thoughts and feelings to occur, so long as we return to the present. No direct focus on the breath (although some version of Mindfulness do, we will not use this step). Not attempting to travel deep within. Just sitting with this conscious experience and the body as well. Truly becoming the observer who witnesses, but does not identify.

How to Practice Mindfulness Meditation

1.) **Sit comfortably.** While the emphasis of this method is awareness of the moment, it doesn't mean centering our focus on just the body, which can inadvertently occur when our posture and positioning are not set prior.

2.) **Breathe Deeply.** Again we will start by allowing the blood to flow at a slightly higher pace, and this is done by taking 5-6 deep breaths once we are seated.

3.) **Chant the affirmation "Thoughts come, thoughts go. I am love, I am whole."** For me personally, the use of affirmations directly influences the direction in which my meditation session will go. In the case of Mindfulness, we are to allow thoughts, no matter what they may be or why they may arise, to receive our recognition before returning to the moment. It is important we do not judge, chastise of get frustrated with this process of letting thoughts flow by. If we allow the chaos of unregulated thoughts to get to us, how will we reach a place so far removed from our ego? By chanting this affirmation, we are reminding ourselves of our true loving nature, and embrace the essence of these 'thoughts' for what they are; merely waves in an ocean of human consciousness. And in order for the waters to smooth, all we must do is cease messing with it. So we will chant this affirmation ten times, slowly, and with full conviction in the words.

4.) **Situate your awareness in the moment.** With judgement and worry cast aside, all we do now is stay with the moment for however long we feel the need to. Just sitting and witnessing. This is where this meditation takes place. Remaining in the moment mindfully in this case means being mindful not just with our thoughts, but on a sensory level too. You are here and with this, being here now means you will likely hear noises or feel sensations in the body physically as well. All we do is acknowledge and return to this moment, and to stillness. Sounds pop up? Acknowledge and return. Elbow begins to itch? Acknowledge and return. We simply watch these thought and feelings arise, then return to the moment. In doing so we will also gain the ability to witness them fade away.

5.) **Use your breath to remain present.** As is a common theme in most meditation methods, we will use the breath to remain mindful of the eternal moment that is now. In essence, for mindfulness meditation to work we need to have in mind a one-pointed focus so that all other occurrences may fade away, instead of distract us. For this practice we will follow the breath to keep us in this moment. We can do this by either **A.)** directing our awareness to the rising and falling of the abdomen right below the middle of our ribs. This area produces a very subtle sensation of rising and falling that in my opinion is the easiest to witness without becoming hyper-focused on it. Or we may **B.)** center our awareness on the tip of the nose, for when we exhale through it, there is usually a small sensation we can feel as the air leaves us.

6.) **Remain in this space of one-pointed focus.** We now stay with the breath for as long is needed. And that is the beauty of this meditation. Witness, experience, but do not associate with it, and the True-Self will appear. We

7.) **When peace surrounds you, return to the world.** The final step is the 'reward', so to speak, of mindfulness because from here the meditation goes on as long as needed.

The simplicity speaks for itself as does the experience. Sit down, cast away judgement, witness reality as an eternal moment and remain in the now by following the breath until you begin to feel inner peace flowing through your body. This truly is meditation 101 and so for the absolute beginner I would highly suggest you initiate this method.

Chapter 6
Scanning Meditation

We've now explored methods of meditation that focus on diving into silence, and diving into the breath as a center for the witness to observe, and now we move on to one that is situated specifically on the body and the external world as a means for awakening the bliss within each us. This method known as Scanning is a much more recent form of meditation and is exactly what the name implies. We simply scan the body and scan our senses with a vantage of pure awareness, reading each sensory experience from an unidentified perspective. Sounds as sounds. Not as 'us' hearing sounds. Bodily sensations as just that. Not as 'us' feeling a sensation. Separate but aware is the basis of watching these occurrences play out. In doing so one can often awaken a response of *satori,* or seeing our true nature simply by seeing everything else without judgement or personalized perception. This can take years or can be done after only a few sessions of fully integrated scanning. For in the words of Swami Saraswati,

"Control of the senses means control of the mind and ensures perfect safety and supreme peace. Control of one's thoughts leads to control of the mind and senses and to the attainment of infinite bliss and eternal life."

I've noticed during my time practicing as well that scanning more often works for those of us who are overly focused on the body. Whether this comes from drug usage, working out, sexual encounters, personal insecurities and so forth.

Many of us are drawn in life towards the pleasures of the body. This is understandable, because as we spoke of earlier many of us picked up this book not just to still the mind, but because we've heard that meditation just plain *feels* good and might be able to help us accept who we are. If this applies to you, Scanning is an amazing way not just to *feel* our way into meditation, but to wring out that need for physical stimulation from the meditative process itself. Scanning shows us that yes, these are sensations, that we do inhabit a body but again, that it is just a body, while we as a Soul are eternal.

So, if one can inhabit a space beyond their ego's desire to cling to such sensations, they can harvest true awareness and find true happiness within again, showing us that bliss is our true nature, instead of letting the media, our bosses or others individuals the majority of which are misled by the system they are raised within telling us what they find to be true.

How to Practice Scanning Meditation

1.)   **Sit or lay down, wearing comfy clothes.** As this is a meditation on the senses, comfort is very important to expanding our senses and witnessing all of the sensory occurrences around us.

2.)   **Breathe in and out deeply, while counting to fifteen.** In order to heighten the senses, we must get the blood flowing through the body with more oxygen than usual. To do this we will sit with our eyes closed, hands in our lap, and take fifteen deep breaths in through the nose and out through the mouth. Each breath allows the mind to go blank, and only focus on counting the breaths. Inhale, exhale, one. Inhale, exhale, two. And so on until we reach our fifteenth breath.

3.)   **On the fifteenth breath hold in a large gulp of air and suck in the abdomen/stomach.** With the blood now flowing we will hold in the last breath, taking in as much air as possible then sucking in the stomach. At this point imagine all this energy within being condensed and becoming heavier throughout the entire body. This will give us a far greater awareness, from fingers to toes, than we are usually aware of physically.

4.)   **Exhale deeply and begin scanning the body as the witness.** We now begin the process of scanning. As with prior meditations, allow the breath to rise and fall on its own accord while we sit in a space beyond the body, as the witness. And as the witness, we are simply watching the sensations of the body. We do this first by starting at the crown of our head, and slowly over the course of thirty to sixty seconds, scanning all the way

71

down to our toes for about twenty minutes. Simply watch the sensations that arise when we focus on the head, face neck, then shoulders and so on, all the way down the body. At first we will often want to identify each area of the body we are feeling. "My head, my elbows, my thighs" etc. The magic of scanning is just learning *not to do this at all*. All we are is the witness, which is nothing. There is no witness! Only pure awareness. So scan the body as one thing. An example of this would be when looking at a square. We don't analyze a square and say, "Top left corner. Top right corner. Bottom right corner. Bottom left corner." All we say is "Square." We see it as one thing. So too must we view this vessel as just the body as our scanning deepens. Over time you will notice that your ability to scan from top to bottom will cease to include the names of the alleged areas you are scanning! This is when satori experiences will arise as the soul, and ego as well, begin to truly recognize in an "Ah-ha!" moment that our true nature is not the body. And thusly we awaken inner peace.

5.)   **Move from witnessing the body, to witnessing the external world as what you are**. For the first few weeks of Scanning, this step is one I recommend be skipped until we can step away from constantly identifying with the body. However once breakthroughs begin to occur and we can see our true nature isn't the organism, or just our conscious experience, we can move on. So once we meditate on the bodily experiences for twenty minutes, slowly begin to shift your focus to the senses provided through what you smell and what you hear. The senses of taste and sight are irrelevant to this practice as the eyes should remain closed, and hopefully we are not eating during this meditation. At this point we probably have an image of the room we are in, the house we are in and the city where we live as well.

All we do now is continue to expand our awareness as all of this being what we are. Simply rising and falling with the breath as the whole of reality moving to this beat.

6.) **Watch your sensory experiences, but do not identify with them.** Much like with the body, all we are doing as the witness is watching what our senses pick up on with loving awareness, but not classifying them or trying to identify them. And even if we do (as will be common for beginners), just remind yourself that whatever definition you just used is not true and return to complete awareness. The satori experiences of scanning externally too become very extreme in their reactions because over time, as we begin to watch external reality without any form of judgement, the lines between what the ego sees as 'me' and 'the world' begin to disappear. From within we will realize not only intellectually but experientially that there is no self that is separate from the whole. In that moment we become aware that all is one. Again we will see that, "*I AM.*" This is the power of sensory scanning.

7.) **Embrace the whole in which you are & Return** Each session of scanning will bring us closer and closer to the truth aforementioned. And after roughly half an hour of this practice, upon opening our eyes. You will now open them as bliss incarnate. And before standing up or returning to your identity, your plans, or to thoughts of your next meal, remind yourself five to ten times silently of your nature as the witness, and the whole. As nothing but loving awareness beyond all form. Then go play out your form!

With this we have completed the highly powerful experience of scanning meditation. And over time can hopefully learn to see beyond out insecurities our anchors currently tying us to our physical forms.

Chapter 7
Mantra Meditation

Our penultimate meditative practice is by far the most ancient religious method, known in Hinduism as *Mantra Japa* or simply to us as Mantra Meditation. This meditation centers around a spoken *mantra* either out loud or within our mind, for the word mantra itself very roughly translates to 'repetitive mental tool' and according to A.C Bhaktivedanta Swami Prabdupada,

> "The *mantra* is the tool which delivers the mind from speculation on it's true nature."

To put it simply, a *mantra* is a pure, intention-based word or saying that when repeated continuously, allows the mind to enter into transcendental bliss or supreme realization in the same way watching the breath or scanning the body did in our earlier methods. Mantra originally translates from (*mana*) as mind, and (*tra*) as a vehicle or instrument. Therefore, a mantra is an instrument for the mind to use in meditative practice.

The history of mantras and their powers is one spanning over 6,000 years and of course, in such an extensive span of time deepening on which school of Hinduism one followed, determined the method of mantra meditation they followed. Much like the scanning method, Mantra Meditation is active rather than passive, in that instead of attempting to quiet the mind with focus the action of chanting itself will quiet the mind for us. As we chant this word or saying, there becomes less and less room for other thoughts to invade the mind, and soon we enter a space of one-pointedness where only the mantra exists. Not only that it alone exists, but in becoming aware of this one word as all of reality in that moment, we will be doing so from the space of ego-silence the prior-mentioned methods are also attempting to get us too. This is the power of the mantra, it transcends personality and with it attain inner peace, bliss and love for the mantra as reality itself. Only upon ceasing the mantra do we snap back into personality and remember, "Wow. So that is how far out of my own sense of self one-pointedness can take me." This method too is great for those of us who may have trouble sitting in silence as the first two methods advise. For me personally Mantra meditation was and is, other than Insight, my go-to method of meditation due to the malleability of the practice. While for the sake of simplicity we will be sitting down, in time chanting can be done with friends or alone when walking around, or while engaged with the external world too. This makes it the only meditation in this manual that can be done anywhere, at virtually any place with results we can witness in real time. So for simplicity's sake this simple method requires only two tools that allow us to practice *Mantra Japa*, repetitive chanting of the mantra to awaken us all from the world of *Maya* we currently believe we are a part of.

Mantra Meditation Tools

1.) **Japa/Mala Beads.** Japa beads are a collection of beads, knotted together by string between each bead, traditionally having 108 beads and a guru bead. Historically one will begin and end their practice on the guru bead, which represents the full encapsulation of the mantra we are using, or can represent the universe as a whole in the palm of our hand. Helping us conceptualize that reality is everything and that everything, even a small bead, is in turn the entire universe... These beads are used throughout Vaishnavism and other sects of Hinduism by beginners and advanced practitioners alike. I would recommend using either sandalwood mala beads, or Rudraksha mala beads due to their sacred association in Hindu theology.

2.) **Japa/Mala Bag.** This is simply a small cloth pouch to hold our beads while we meditate on the mantra we choose. While I and many other practitioners may wear Japa beads around their neck or wrists, holding them in a Japa bag, especially when meditating is done so that our beads remain cared for, clean, and impossible to drop or lose. I compare this to when getting an expensive phone those who truly care and understand the importance of the phone will use a case to protect it. Much the same these *Japa* beads are our physical key to a conscious awakening. Do we treat such a life-altering tool with disrespect? Throwing it on the ground or holding it in dirty hands? Well I would hope not. By practicing mindfulness and gratefulness for this spiritual tool, we express that externally by making sure they are clean and protected so a clear and loving intention can always rest within our own mind when we pick them up for use.

As with anything, the variations of mantras are endless. There are Buddhist mantras, Hindu mantras, and self-empowerment mantras dating back millenniums. All work, all are correct. It just depends on which mantra synchronizes with our soul the most effectively. As we chant, all we must watch for is which words feel like just plain words, and which words feel like the language of eternity? That is how we discover the mantra meant for us.

How to Practice Mantra Meditation

1.) **Decide upon your mantra (Trial and Error).** This will be the first tool in this meditation, however know that once you have discovered your mantra, this step is no longer needed. For those with no knowledge of Hindu or Buddhist mantras, thousands exist only a quick Google search away! Or if a temple exists nearby where you live, there are many well versed teachers who would gladly assist you in finding a few that suit your own personal awakening practice.

2.) **Sit down and get comfortable.** Once again, the less we worry about the body, the easier we awaken oneness through pure focus on the mantra.

3.) **Place your right hand in your Japa bag and grasp the guru bead.** At this point sitting comfortably, we will begin by placing our right hand inside of our Japa bag. When doing this our index finger will stick out the small hole on the opposite side of the Japa bag from where our hand enters. This is due to the pointer finger often being seen as an 'accusatory' finger because of our use of it when we point at people or chastise people by waving it. This means that our Japa beads will rest between the thumb and middle finger, with the placement of the bag in the middle of our lap. With the right hand seated with Japa in the lap, rest your left hand comfortable on the left knee as it will not be needed.

4.)   **Perform the following steps to practice Mantra Japa correctly:** This step is comprised of a few methods that all interact together to perform the practice of mantra meditation. If we do this smoothly and in sequence, they will in time become one continuous fluid movement, instead of breaking them down now for a simpler understanding. **Inhale.** Breathe in softly through the nose. **Chant the mantra (either out loud or in your mind).** Where exhaling quietly would be in other methods, we instead will chant the mantra, which acts as an exhalation itself. **While chanting focus the mantra on the bead in your hand.** We are using the mantra to attain mental stillness, as we do this we are seeing the bead currently in our hand as the mantra itself. The mantra is ultimate reality. The bead is the mantra. This means that the bead too is the universe in our palm, and that we are one with it. **As the mantra ends use your thumb to reach forward and pull the next bead into a resting position between thumb and middle finger.** All we do here is wait for the last moment of the mantra, or until directly after the mantra has ended to reach for the next bead. **Repeat these steps again.** And thusly we repeat the process 108 times, which is known as completing a full round of Japa. This is mantra meditation.

5.)   **Remember to chant with love.** Love is the true nature of awareness, for True Consciousness is *ananda*, which appears as unconditional love in the human form. Therefore, we must remember to truly place our heart and soul into the mantra as we chant it. Surrender all that you are, all that you perceive yourself to be, to the mantra as if it was all that existed in the world. For in this moment it is. If we just mumble mantras uninterestedly 108 times nothing will happen but us opening our eyes and saying, "Wow saying that word for so long did nothing." And this is only due to lack of intention behind our actions in this scenario. Yet if we chant with love, beyond conditions, we will emerge from Mantra Japa with tears of joy in our eyes from the wisdom of realizing our oneness with all things that chanting will provide to us.

6.) **Upon reaching the guru bead, flip the mala around and go back the other direction.** When starting some of us may chant slowly, meaning one round of 108 mantras can extend roughly fifteen to twenty minutes. But if you reach the end of your first round, feel the guru bead is back in your hands but want to keep chanting, it is customary not to cross over the guru bead. For we cannot transcend the guru, which is reality itself. We are subject to the experience of it. So to represent this we surrender to the universe, to the guru, and instead of attempting to bypass it, we merely turn around the beads in our hand and begin to chant 108 rounds back the other way. This is a great tool for humbling ourselves that is so small and simple it will in time, excite us to reach the guru bead, surrender our ego to it, and turn around to begin again.

7.) **Chant until blissed out, or until the round amount you set is reached.** As with most meditation, the time we sit and awaken peace is not limited, so it is up to us to decide how long we chant for. Some might chant one round, others chant ten. In truth, it really is just up to us to set a parameter before begging.

By the time we end, however, you will know the soul is awake for there will be virtually no thoughts in the mind to return to. All we feel is peace, which is also a fabulous means of measuring just how well each mantra works for us and whether or not it needs to be altered so that we really may see our true nature.

This divine game of chanting is a meditative method unlike any other. So on a final note I will add that if all else fails, and you are chanting quietly, begin chanting out loud and vice versa! As Swami Muktananda would often lecture, the beauty of Mantra Meditation is that it is one of a select few meditative methods than can be done out loud and therefore done in situations of multiple people, or public places. Muktananda would say his explanation for this is that the external mantra is an outward expression of our internal loving nature, living as a soul. Because even if we don't mean to, or are unaware of it, we are making noises which in turn vibrates the air and objects in close proximity to us. These vibrations plant subconscious seeds of awakening in them! More beautiful still is that much like singing, chanting with one or more other souls means we can harmonize mantras making the experience of awaking far more intense and in synch.

On the other side when we chant within our mind we are chanting to the our True- Self which is the *Atman*! So either we are vibrating the hearts of others, or vibrating our own heart. This is what makes *Mantra Japa* equally powerful for sages and students alike. Holding the world in the palm of our hand, while we come to see that we are *the world* in which we hold. Mantra meditation more than any prior method is renowned for its ability cut through the current illusions of separation between body and soul. It instead shines a light upon their interconnected nature in regards to the human form!

Chapter 7

Zazen

(Zen Meditation)

On a final meditative note we reach Zazen, or the Zen method of meditation. This is the shortest, most obscure method of meditation compared to the rest of our practices. According to many Zen masters over the last few thousand years it creates the wisest of souls, who can awaken at any moment, but that such an awakening is not something one who practices Zazen can predict or plan for.

Zazen translates directly to 'Sitting Meditation' and that alone is what Zen Meditation is. As we spoke of before, the deepest layer of meditation is that of Pure Consciousness, which is true silent self. Zen does not feed into the idea of souls, or of any of the prior meditative practices as working whatsoever. It doesn't even entertain the idea of souls as something that might exist. On the simplest of levels all Zen cares about is understanding that there is 'one mind' and that is all of reality. It is not in any way shape or form, consciously aware. It simply *is* pure awareness. Thusly we are as well. So if this space does not exist, and cannot be accessed, why practice Zen?

This is why many spiritualists may find Zen a ridiculous practice due to it having no fruits or ways of benefiting the ego-self, which oddly enough it exactly why people do it. Zen exists for the purpose of dropping our roles and sinking into the same awareness we held before taking up the human form. Silence.

We don't 'experience' Zen. We don't get anything from it unless our ego-self incorrectly perceives an experience as 'ours'. Instead we sit just to sit. We allow the mind to go blank with no ulterior motive, which is something most people rooted in their identity can never or would never want to do. Especially if, like most of us here, we *want* inner peace and *want* to access new spiritual insights. In Zen, by just sitting we get used to the practice of letting the mind go blank and simply being here with the direct experience, with nothing to take from it. The more one does this, the farther they can go with this shut-off mind. Over years one begins to open their eyes, leave the room, and even partake in daily activities without thinking a single thought. This is truly the deepest art of living in the moment. But rest assured, unlike the previous methods, Zazen does not come easy. Most changes take many years to awaken. As a child it is easy to act without thought. As an adult who has learned to think his way through life, reverting to a childlike state, known in Zen as *shoshin* or having a beginner's mind, is much more difficult. A common theme in Zen is that it is achieved by, "Thinking of not thinking."

This sounds paradoxical but know this, there is only one way of achieving this state, and it is indeed by not thinking. This is the method of Zen meditation we will now practice known as *Shikantaza,* or as it roughly translates to in Japanese, 'just sitting.' Because at its core, this method of Zazen really isn't anything else but sitting with it all. Not focusing internally. Not focusing externally. It's just sitting in this moment, and seeing this moment for what it is

An eternal moment.

How to Practice Zazen

1.)   **Sit down and get comfortable.** As always, comfort provides less distraction. In Zazen this is done most commonly with the meditator sitting on a *zafu* (small round cushion) which in turn rests upon a *zabuton* or cushioned mat. These are simply to provide maximum comfort due to many practitioners of Zazen sitting for multiple hour sessions.

2.)   **Sit about one foot from the nearest wall and face towards it.** While not fully necessary to practice this meditation method, it is the most popular method used currently in Zen monasteries since it was introduced by *Bodhidharma,* the first patriarch of Ch'an (the original, Chinese religion that was followed by Japan's Zen later on. When asked about this practice of wall sitting, he once replied,

"Those who turn from delusion back to reality, who meditate on walls, the absence of self and other... Who remain unmoved even by scriptures are in complete and unspoken agreement with reason."

Reason, in this sense is expressed as middle ground within the mind. As *Upekkha* or equanimity and peace of mind as it translates to from Pali. This is where D.T Suzuki, the 20th century's foremost voice on Zen would often express the wall as a reflection of the mind. The wall we sit in front of stands straight, unmoving and unflinching in its ability to *be as it is*. And although our eyes will be closed, by sitting directly in front of a wall we know that as we sit, our reflection of allowing the mind to be free and reside in an unflinching state of peace exists too in the sturdiness the wall directly in front of us.

3.) **Empty the mind and allow thoughtlessness to fill you.** From here all we do is sit. Allow thoughts to come and go until thoughtlessness becomes our reality and we may sit with it for hours on end. This is all Zazen is. Sitting. Watching. Allowing thoughtlessness to be what we are. But for those who just can't seem to shake their thoughts, a great method for beginners is by thinking of what thoughtlessness would be like. In essence, using reverse psychology in our mind to instantly initiate a faux-thoughtless experience. Just to get a tiny taste of it, so that we can return to sitting and allow such a state to eventually appear on its own.

4.) **When returning don't let ego judge your session afterwards.** Don't think about it. Just practice then move on. Open your eyes after about an hour of meditating or however long you felt like sitting, and simply stay with *upekkha* as you return to your identity and the tasks you have in the real world. This is how Zazen over years can fully rewire the mind of it's practitioner. Over decades it potentially allows one to quite easily enter a state of *nirvana*, or a space of living without any form of suffering whatsoever. For if we are just here, unmoving in our awareness yet loving, in time we see the ever-moving current of existence itself. And when we see this in every moment, our practice of Zazen reminds us never to attach or expect anything from it. This is the beauty of Zazen. Sit and become as stable as the wall. For as it is often said in the Soto practice, "Zen is."

So we will leave it at that.

Chapter 8
Epilogue

Guiding Ourselves & Others

Although you've always been here, now hopefully you've truly arrived. Above we hold paths within, paths without, paths of chanting and paths of doing, well, nothing at all really. Where they lead you will for a while be up to your ego-self and just how dedicated it is to awakening oneness, and recognizing the eternal master in which it has always been. While beginning meditation might be hard, eventually it will become simple. Nothing worth having comes easy. Meditation might not be fun either, but as we should know by now that shouldn't matter. Brushing our teeth isn't exactly fun is it? And yet we still know that doing it assists us in life. Meditation is quite the same. Still, if you ever find yourself in doubt, never forget that you can always seek out wisdom from other books, as well as teachers in the real world. Meditation is continuously rising in popularity in the Western world and with it one can find temples, shalas, rooms and retreats for all the forms listed above with a simple Google search and some quick reading.

I currently teach meditation in Los Angeles, but when I'm not I remain forever the student of my elders and attend the guided sessions of other teachers when my schedule permits it. The presence of a teacher helps tremendously and you may find, as millions already do, that sitting in a room with a dozen or more living souls also meditating can make the experience that much stronger and that much easier to practice as we are not at home alone with just our own ego judging every move, and can thusly drop our 'spiritual guard' so to speak. You are already whole. You are already aware. All you must do is remember.

With the passing of time however, one warning I will give before wrapping this manual up is not to jump too quickly into trying to teach others directly from your own experience. Often when we notice or assume we are finally 'mastering' a form of meditation, it is really just the ego in drag using spirituality as an accomplishment. This is as far from the intended goal of meditation as one can get. I personally spent over five years meditating alone in my room, jumping between methods, before ever transferring my own practices into that of guidance for others. Even then part of me felt, maybe wait another five years?

Instead, it is best we trust teachers and those with far more experience with these practices if we find ourselves around friends or family who may be interested in meditating. While we may assume we *totally get it,* there is no harm in humbling ourselves and allowing a more experienced soul to provide them their tools.

So due in part to my young age, I will again mention that this is merely the manual which has been produced from my experience and from my masters. For more information and detailed practices, I would advise you to seek the works of Adyashanti, David Nichtern, Joan Halifax, Swami Adiswarananda, S.N Goenka and Ramana Maharshi, to name a few trusted teachers.

Inside is Outside

Meditation saves lives, vanquishes the regressive aspects of ego that have built up over the course of our own lives and above all, reminds us that we are (as the Vedas put it), the Eternal. Pure Consciousness. Love. Bliss. Forever. We are just playing out this game of ephemeral existence for a few decades before we return.

You can run from this truth, deny it and attempt to use scientific theories to navigate around it, but the moment you sit down & look within, this eternal truth will undoubtedly arise. It has done so for thousands of years & so long as meditative practices exist it will continue to awaken all that embrace it. You are here now. The True-Self is waiting to be revealed and a mentality of peace is anticipating cultivation to assist us as we live out our lives. Once again I will remind you;

Tat Tvam Asi!
Though art that!
The whole of reality!
That is what you are!
Go remember it!

Ram Ram
- Koi Fresco

91

52870226R10057

Made in the USA
Middletown, DE
22 November 2017